21st Century Christianity

David Self

HODDER
Wayland

an imprint of Hodder Children's Books

First published in 2005 by Hodder Wayland,
an imprint of Hodder Children's Books

© Hodder Wayland 2005

Subject consultant: Jane Clements, The Council of Christians
and Jews
Project Editor, Hodder Wayland: Kirsty Hamilton
Editor: Nicola Barber
Designer: Janet McCallum
Picture Researcher: Shelley Noronha, Glass Onion Pictures
Maps and artwork: Peter Bull

British Library Cataloguing Publication Data
Self, David
Christianity – (21st century religions)
1. Christianity – Juvenile literature
I. Title
230

ISBN 0750247061

Colour Reproduction by Dot Gradations Ltd, UK
Printed in China

Hodder Children's Books
A division of Hodder Headline Limited
338 Euston Road, London NW1 3BH

The publisher would like to thank the following for permission to
reproduce their pictures: The Art Archive 11 Niedersachsisches
Museum, 13 Archaeological Museum Spalato/Dagli Orti (A);
Bridgeman Art Library www.bridgeman.co.uk/Galleria dell'
Accademia, Florence, Italy 8, Stapleton Collection, UK 9, Bibliotheque
Municipale, Moulins, France/Lauros/Giraudon 17, Sant' Apollinare
Nuovo, Ravenna, Italy/Giraudon 18, National Library, St Petersburg,
Russia 21, Hotel Dieu, Beaune, France/Paul Maeyaert 41; Robert
Harding Picture Library/ J.P. De Mann 7, J. Greenberg 16, Travel
Library 30, M. Jenner 31, ASAP 32, R. Francis 33, I. Talby 34, N.
Wheeler 35, S. Grandadam 37, B. Barbier 43; Hutchison Picture
Library 40; Alex Keene 25; Ann and Bury Peerless 24, 29; Rex
Pictures Ltd/Ilyas J. Dean 5, Sipa 14; Topfoto 19, 20, 22, 23, 26, 27,
28, 38, 39, 44, 45

weblinks

You don't need a computer to use this book. But, for readers who do have access to the Internet, the book provides links to recommended websites which offer additional information and resources on the subject.

You will find weblinks boxes like this on some pages of the book.

weblinks

For more information about Christianity, go to www.waylinks.co.uk/ series/21stcentury/Christianity

waylinks.co.uk

To help you find the recommended websites easily and quickly, weblinks are provided on our own website, **waylinks.co.uk.** These take you straight to the relevant websites and save you typing in the Internet address yourself.

Internet safety

↗ Never give out personal details, which include: your name, address, school, telephone number, email address, password and mobile number.

↗ Do not respond to messages which make you feel uncomfortable – tell an adult.

↗ Do not arrange to meet in person someone you have met on the Internet.

↗ Never send your picture or anything else to an online friend without a parent's or teacher's permission.

↗ If you see anything that worries you, tell an adult.

A note to adults
Internet use by children should be supervised. We recommend that you install filtering software which blocks unsuitable material.

Website content

The weblinks for this book are checked and updated regularly. However, because of the nature of the Internet, the content of a website may change at any time, or a website may close down without notice. While the Publishers regret any inconvenience this may cause readers, they cannot be responsible for the content of any website other than their own.

HODDER
Wayland

Contents

Note

Christians number years as either BC ('Before Christ') or AD ('*Anno Domini*' – Latin for 'In the year of our Lord'). In this book, however, years are described as being either BCE ('Before the Common Era') or CE ('Common Era'). The year numbers are the same in both methods.

The Russian monk who created the AD method of numbering the years, in the 6th century CE, miscalculated the probable year of Jesus' birth. We now believe that Jesus was more likely to have been born around the years 7 to 4BCE.

Introduction

Christianity began about two thousand years ago, when a man called Jesus lived in Nazareth, a town that lay in the district of Galilee. Jesus worked as a carpenter, or possibly as a builder, until he was thirty years old. He never went to college. He never wrote a book. He never travelled very far outside his own country. For just three years he wandered around Galilee teaching. A number of friends followed him. He journeyed south to the main city of that region, Jerusalem, which is now in the country we call Israel. There, one of his twelve closest followers betrayed him. He went through a series of trials and was found innocent. Even so, he was condemned and put to death by being crucified on a cross.

▼ *Jesus told his followers to take his message to all the nations of the world. Two thousand years later, Christians can indeed be found all around the world.*

weblinks

For ideas about where to look for more information about Christianity, go to www.waylinks.co.uk/series/21stcentury/Christianity

Jesus today

Although all of this happened about two thousand years ago, Jesus' teachings have not been forgotten. Today he has about 2,000 million followers worldwide, forming the largest religion in the modern world. These followers are called Christians. They believe that Jesus was fully human and experienced the pains and joys of life in the same way that other people did in his time. But they also believe that Jesus was the Son of God.

By this, Christians mean that God became a human being, living on earth as Jesus Christ (sometimes called the Son of God) to save human beings from the results of their wrongdoings ('sins') and disobedience. The word Christ is not a name but a title, meaning 'the anointed one' or 'the chosen one'. The Hebrew word for this is 'Messiah'. Jesus has been known to his followers as the Messiah since the time he was alive on earth.

Christian belief

Although Jesus died on the cross when he was crucified, for Christians this is not the end of the story. They believe that three days later he rose from the dead and was seen and touched by his followers. Eventually, he returned to his Father in heaven. Even that was not the end. According to Christians, God then sent his Holy Spirit to earth to 'comfort' (the word originally meant 'to make strong') all those who follow the teachings of Jesus.

➤ *Young Christians in Azam Basti, Pakistan, remember the crucifixion of Jesus in a Good Friday procession.*

Worship

Christians meet together to worship in churches, chapels or cathedrals. Their holy book is the Bible which contains many shorter books arranged in two sections: the Old Testament (which also forms the holy writings of the Jews) and the New Testament.

Not everyone who calls him or herself a Christian takes part in church services, although worship and prayer are important aspects of life for many Christians. Some Christians simply profess a belief in God the Father, God the Son (Jesus) and God the Holy Spirit. For many, one of the most important elements of being a Christian is to try to follow Jesus' words: 'Love God and love your neighbour as you love yourself.'

1 The growth of Christianity

*C*hristianity began with one man in a small Middle Eastern country which formed a tiny part of the Roman Empire. It has grown into a worldwide faith with believers in every continent around the world. Christians have many differences, but they all believe in the same Jesus Christ and try to follow his teachings.

Jesus the man

Historians agree that Jesus was a real person: he did exist. But apart from a few references to him by Roman historians, all our information about Jesus comes from the writings of his followers. We have no description of what he looked like. It was not until several hundred years after his life that people started making pictures of him. So what do we know about him?

Jesus was a Jew. According to the accounts written by his followers, he was born to Jewish parents in a town called Bethlehem, about ten kilometres south of Jerusalem. Bethlehem was the town where his earthly father, Joseph, had been born. Joseph and Mary, the mother of Jesus, had gone there to take part in a taxation census (count) of all the people in the country. But their home was further north, in a town called Nazareth in part of the country called Galilee.

Jesus grew up in Nazareth. His parents were devout Jews and he went to the local synagogue on the Jewish holy day, or Sabbath (Saturday). He could read and was undoubtedly well-respected because he was asked to read and preach in the synagogue.

➤ *As far as we know, Jesus spent his whole life in what is sometimes called 'the Holy Land', an area that today falls mainly within the boundaries of Israel, Jordan and the Palestinian National Authority.*

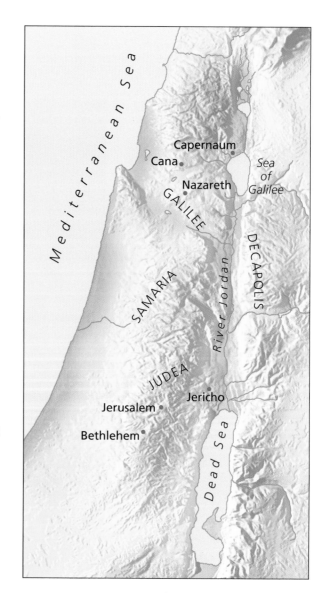

Casting out devils

A miracle is an event that cannot be explained by science. The New Testament contains accounts of many miracles performed by Jesus. Some of them involved curing blind and dumb people. Jesus cured other people by 'casting out devils'. In those days, people did not understand how illnesses were caught and they thought that the air was full of 'devils' trying to inhabit a person. Some Christians have questioned whether these miracles really did happen. Many believe they did – and also that miracle cures can and do still happen.

▲ *This picture of the young Jesus in the arms of his mother is painted on the wall of a church in Ura Kedane Meheriet near Lake Tana, Ethiopia, in Africa.*

Jesus the teacher

When he was about thirty, Jesus chose twelve local men to be his closest followers, or disciples. With them, he spent three years travelling around the country, talking to and teaching the people they met. He became very popular and large crowds came to listen. Some of them brought people who were ill or disabled and Jesus helped or cured many of these people. These acts are called miracles. Jesus performed many miracles, for example one story tells how he fed five thousand people with just a few loaves and fishes. Partly because Jesus was so popular, and partly because of what he taught, some of the religious leaders of the country began to be jealous of him and to plot how they might have him arrested.

Palm Sunday

Having spent three years teaching and healing, Jesus went to Jerusalem. He entered the city riding on a donkey. Many years earlier a Jewish prophet called Zechariah had said that, one day, the King of the Jews would enter Jerusalem riding on an ass (or donkey) and that he would be the Messiah, or deliverer, of the Jews. Large crowds welcomed Jesus, cheering and waving branches of palm trees. This day is now known as Palm Sunday.

Jesus spent the week living with friends in a nearby village called Bethany. Each day he went into Jerusalem and taught in the Temple, the Jews' most holy building. During the week, Judas, one of his disciples, met the Jewish chief priests to betray Jesus.

The Last Supper

On the Thursday evening, Jesus had a special 'last supper' with his disciples. During this supper, he washed the disciples' feet (a sign that he was their servant) and told them to eat bread and drink wine in his memory. This act of sharing bread and wine ('the body and blood of Jesus') is celebrated by Christians whenever they meet to take part in a service of Holy Communion.

Judas later left that 'last supper' to tell the chief priests where their soldiers could arrest Jesus. Jesus and his disciples went into a garden to pray. Judas led the soldiers to the garden and the soldiers arrested Jesus and took him away. Christians now call this day Maundy Thursday.

---

weblinks

For more information about Christianity, go to www.waylinks.co.uk/series/21stcentury/Christianity

---

◄ *For Christians, the Last Supper is one of the most important events in the life of Jesus. This painting is by the 14th-century Italian artist Taddeo Gaddi. Judas is shown without a halo, turning away from Jesus and the other disciples. Artists sometimes paint a halo around a person's head to show that person is in some way holy.*

Good Friday

Jesus was put on trial by the chief priests and accused of blasphemy (preaching against God). But the chief priests did not have the authority to put Jesus to death so they sent him to the Roman Governor of the country, Pontius Pilate. However, Pilate found no fault with Jesus.

By now a mob of Jesus' opponents was calling for his execution. To prevent a riot, Pilate ordered Jesus to be beaten and put to death by being nailed to a wooden cross. This was called crucifixion and was the usual Roman method of executing criminals. After three hours on the cross, Jesus died. His body was taken down and put into a small cave, then a heavy stone was rolled across the entrance. These events happened on the day Christians now call Good Friday.

Resurrection

Early the following Sunday morning, a group of women who had been among Jesus' followers (including Mary his mother) went to the tomb. They found that the stone had been rolled away and, in some accounts, they were told by an angel that Jesus had risen from the dead. Some of them ran to tell the disciples. Although they did not believe the women, two of the disciples called Peter and John went back to the tomb – but they also found it was empty.

Over the next forty days, Jesus appeared on several occasions to different groups of followers. From these accounts, Christians believe that Jesus did indeed rise from the dead – an event they call his Resurrection. Christians believe this means they, too, can have eternal life in heaven.

➤ *The scene of the crucifixion as imagined by the 19th-century German artist, Siegfried Detler Bendixen. Jesus was crucified with two robbers – one on either side. For Christians, the cross on which Jesus died has become the symbol of their faith.*

Pentecost

Seven weeks after the Resurrection, the disciples met in secret in an upstairs room in Jerusalem. The Bible tells us that as they were praying, they heard a sound like 'the rushing of a mighty wind'. They saw what looked like tongues of fire on their heads, but were unharmed. They deduced that a promise Jesus had given them that God would send them his Holy Spirit as a source of strength and comfort had come true.

Led by Peter, they rushed into the streets to preach and to seek converts for the first time. Some of the crowds who heard them thought they were drunk (even though it was early morning). But it is said that three thousand people became Christians that day. For this reason, the day, now known as Pentecost, is sometimes called the birthday of the Church. The disciples continued to preach about Jesus, many of them journeying to other countries. From this time on, the disciples were known as 'apostles', which means 'sent out as messengers'.

The Apostle Paul

Just as the religious leaders in Jerusalem had tried to prevent Jesus from preaching, so they tried to stop the apostles. One young man who was very active in his persecution of Christians was a strict Jew called Saul. But a few years after Jesus' crucifixion, on a journey to a nearby city called Damascus, Saul had a vision of Jesus. He became a follower himself, changed his name to Paul and began to travel widely around the Mediterranean Sea, spreading the teachings of Jesus.

Paul founded many Christian communities in cities of the Roman Empire. He was also the first apostle to preach the Christian faith to gentiles (non-Jews). Paul was finally put on trial for his beliefs, but as he was a Roman citizen as well as a Jew, he claimed the right to be tried in Rome. Paul was executed at about the same time as Peter who had travelled to Rome to spread Jesus' teachings, and who also played a leading role in the early Christian community.

Paul's journeys

Journey	Year (CE)	Destination
First	46-47	What is now southern Turkey and Cyprus
Second	50-52	Turkey (then known as Asia Minor) and Greece
Third	52-56	Many of the places he visited on his first two journeys
Final	60	To Rome, as a prisoner

→ Paul's first journey → Paul's third journey
→ Paul's second journey → Paul's journey to Rome

We know more about Paul than most of the other apostles because he wrote many letters (known as Epistles) to those he had met on his travels. These Epistles contain Paul's teachings about Jesus and survive as part of the New Testament.

▼ *This 15th-century painting from Germany illustrates the moment when Jesus appeared to Saul in a vision, on the road to Damascus. Saul converted to Christianity and changed his name to Paul. He then started to preach the Christian faith to others.*

The spread of the Gospel

The word Gospel means 'good news'. The four books of the New Testament that describe the life and teachings of Jesus are called Gospels. The word is also used to mean the teachings of Christianity – teachings that the apostles began to spread to countries outside the land where Jesus lived. By the year 100CE, there were Christians in many of the towns and cities around the eastern end of the Mediterranean Sea.

From then on, Christians began to teach the Gospel in other parts of the Roman Empire

which (by the year 300CE) stretched from Spain in the west to Jerusalem in the east, northwards to include England and south to the North African coast. By this time there were four great centres of Christianity: Jerusalem, Antioch, Rome and what became known as Constantinople.

The spread of Christianity happened despite the fact that the Romans continued to persecute Christians. Many Christians were put to death by crucifixion, by being fed to lions, and in other ways. This was because Christians would not worship the Roman Emperors (who were said to be holy) or the

▼ *By the year 300CE, Christianity had spread to many countries and cities around the Mediterranean Sea.*

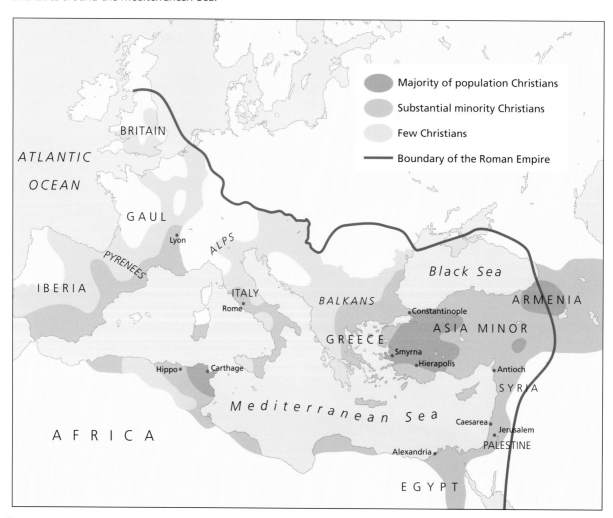

Roman gods. During these early times, being a Christian involved meeting in secret and risking death when spreading the 'good news' or Gospel of Jesus.

Then, in the year 306CE, all this changed. A man called Constantine was proclaimed Emperor of Rome (although he did not actually become emperor until 312). Six years later, he had a vision or dream which was to lead to Christianity becoming the official religion of the Roman Empire (see box).

In the following centuries, the Gospel began to spread through Europe. For example, it was taken to Ireland by the man now known as St Patrick in the 5th century. Gradually the faith began to reach the countries of northern and eastern Europe, converting the people the Romans had called 'barbarians'.

The conversion of Emperor Constantine

In 312CE, the night before he went into battle to win the title Emperor of Rome, Constantine believed Jesus appeared to him in a dream promising victory if Constantine fought under the symbol of the Christian cross. The next day, Constantine and his army won the battle easily. As a result of his vision, Constantine made it legal to be a Christian. In 321CE, he made Sunday a public holiday so Christians could worship on that day. He went on to rebuild the ancient city of Byzantium as his Christian capital, renaming it 'Nova Roma', 'New Rome' although it soon came to be called Constantinople (modern-day Istanbul in Turkey). He was himself baptized shortly before his death in 337CE.

▲ *This carving of Constantine on his stone coffin lid shows him holding the Christian cross.*

Divisions in the family

As the Christian Church grew throughout the Roman Empire and beyond, and as the number of believers increased, its leaders tried to make sure that Christians all believed the same things. Even so, Christians in different parts of the world began to hold slightly different beliefs and to organize themselves separately. In particular, differences developed between the Christian Churches in Rome and Constantinople. Eventually, in 1054CE, the two Churches officially split (known as the 'schism'). The western half became what we know today as the Roman Catholic Church based in Rome. The eastern half became the Orthodox group of Churches. The word 'orthodox' means 'true' or 'right'. The Orthodox Churches were (and still are) those found in Greece, Russia and other Eastern European countries.

Church

The word 'church' has three meanings. It can mean all Christians, the whole 'family' of believers. It can also mean a large, separately organized group of Christians who think particular parts of the Christian faith are especially important, for example the Roman Catholic Church or the Baptist Church. And it can mean a building in which Christian worship is practised.

▼ *Pope John Paul II, leader of the Roman Catholic Church at the start of the 21st century, meets members of his Church.*

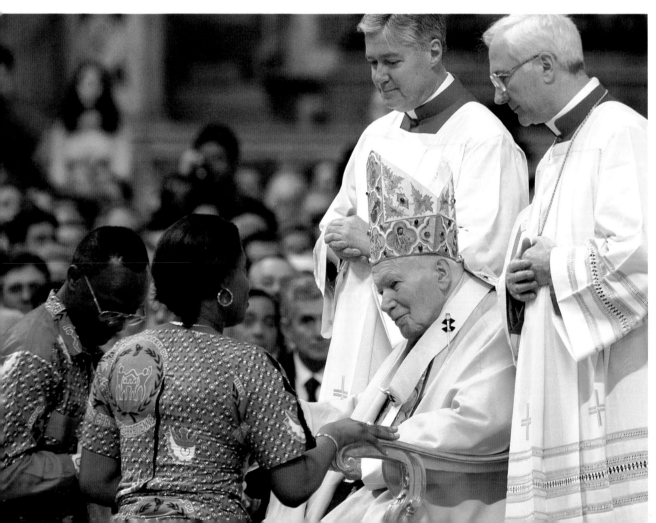

The Roman Catholic Church

About half the Christians in the world now belong to the Roman Catholic Church. 'Catholic' means universal. Roman Catholics trace their history back to the apostle Peter who was the first leader or bishop of the Christians in Rome. Since Peter, the Bishop of Rome has been known as the Pope.

In the centuries following the split between the Catholic and Orthodox Churches, the Roman Catholic Church became very powerful. The Pope was very influential and frequently instructed kings and queens how they should rule. The Church did many good things, but as it became increasingly involved in politics and increasingly wealthy, some people began to question its power and wealth. Many people also wanted the Bible to be printed in their own languages rather than in Latin, the language of the Roman Empire, and the language used for holy texts in the Roman Catholic Church.

The Reformation

In the 16th century, some people (such as a German monk called Martin Luther and a Frenchman called John Calvin) wanted to reform the Church. The quarrel between the reformers and the Church resulted in brutal wars, cruel persecution – and another division. This time of conflict and change became known as the Reformation, and those 'protesters' who left the Roman Church were called Protestants. In England, the Church was reformed but kept some of the customs of the Catholic Church and is known as the Church of England (or Anglican Church). In the centuries that followed, the Protestant and Anglican Churches again divided into separate denominations, or different kinds of Protestantism, such as the Baptists, Methodists and Pentecostals.

---

weblinks

For more information about the Roman Catholic and Methodist churches, go to
www.waylinks.co.uk/series/21stcentury/Christianity

The family of Christian churches

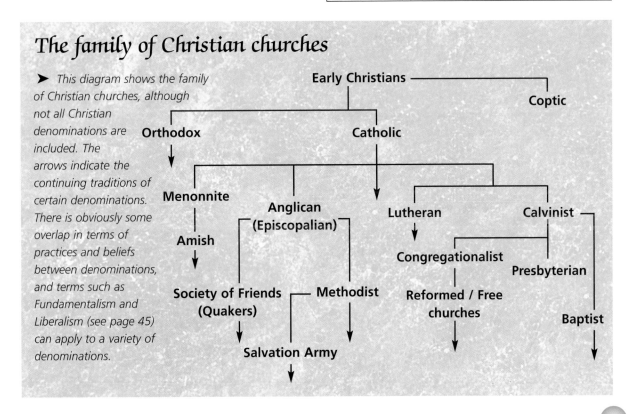

➤ This diagram shows the family of Christian churches, although not all Christian denominations are included. The arrows indicate the continuing traditions of certain denominations. There is obviously some overlap in terms of practices and beliefs between denominations, and terms such as Fundamentalism and Liberalism (see page 45) can apply to a variety of denominations.

Early Christians

Coptic

Orthodox — Catholic

Menonnite — Anglican (Episcopalian) — Lutheran — Calvinist

Amish — Congregationalist — Presbyterian

Society of Friends (Quakers) — Methodist — Reformed / Free churches — Baptist

Salvation Army

2 Christian beliefs and teachings

For many Christians, especially Protestants, faith is built upon the Bible: this holy book is central to what they believe. For others, the teachings of the Church are of similar importance.

The Christian Bible

The Christian Bible contains the complete Jewish Bible, which Christians call the Old Testament. It was written in Hebrew and is made up of 39 separate books including histories, law books, poetry, prophecies, songs and stories.

The second part of the Bible, known as the New Testament, contains 27 books written during the hundred years following the death of Jesus. None was written in his lifetime and they were all written in Greek, the language spoken in most countries around the eastern end of the Mediterranean. The complete Bible was later translated into Latin. Only after the Reformation (see page 15) was it translated into other languages.

The New Testament

The earliest surviving Christian writings are the Epistles (letters) that Paul wrote to the Christian communities he founded around the

▼ Two teenage Christians study the Bible together in North Haledon, New Jersey, in the United States.

Mediterranean (see pages 10-11). In these letters, Paul says little about the life of Jesus but writes more about what Jesus' life, death and Resurrection (and his teachings) mean to Christians. Parts are not easy to understand because Paul was answering letters which have since been lost. The New Testament also contains Epistles thought to have been written by Peter, John and other apostles.

The first four books printed in the New Testament are the Gospels which were mainly written after Paul's Epistles – possibly as late as 70CE. They provide our only accounts of the life of Jesus. The first and fourth Gospels are said to have been written under the names of Matthew and John, and some Christians believe that these were two of Jesus' original disciples. The second is called St Mark's Gospel and was probably the first to be written. Mark may have known Peter who told him about Jesus.

The third Gospel is said to have been written by Luke, a Greek doctor. He was a friend of Paul and he may have been a Greek-speaking Jew, or a gentile. He is also the writer of another New Testament book, the Acts of the Apostles, which describes the early years of the Church.

The last book of the New Testament is called the Revelation of St John and is a series of poetic visions of how God will finally put right all the wrongs and troubles of the world.

▼ Before printing was invented, Christians made handwritten copies of the Bible, often decorating them with pictures of Bible stories. This page from a 12th-century French Bible shows the creation of the world, ending with Adam and Eve in the Garden of Eden (bottom right).

The teachings of Jesus

Jesus taught among other things that the poor, not the rich, are favoured by God, saying: 'Blessed are the poor for theirs is the Kingdom of God.' It was such unexpected ideas that made his message seem revolutionary to many who heard him – and was one reason why such large crowds came to listen to him teach. It was also why some rulers felt threatened by Jesus' teachings.

Many of Jesus' teachings survive in the four Gospels, but each writer selected different ones. Matthew collected many of Jesus' sayings together to form what is called the Sermon on the Mount. (There may well have been an actual occasion when Jesus spoke from a hillside to a particularly large crowd.) In the Sermon on the Mount, Jesus taught that loving and worshipping God involved trying to do what God wants for you. This includes not only 'loving your neighbour' but loving and forgiving your enemies. Jesus said that anyone who did these things would be part of 'the Kingdom of God' or 'the Kingdom of Heaven'.

Included in the Sermon on the Mount are some of the sayings that surprised his listeners. These sayings (in which Jesus stated what people should do to be happy or 'blessed') are called the Beatitudes:

- 'Blessed are the meek for they shall inherit the earth.'

- 'Blessed are you that hunger now, for you shall be satisfied.'

- 'Blessed are you when men … persecute you and utter all kinds of evil against you falsely … for your reward is great in heaven.' (Matthew, chapter 5, verses 5, 6, 11-12)

▼ *This 6th-century mosaic from a church in Ravenna, Italy, shows Jesus preaching his Sermon on the Mount.*

➤ *This illustration of the parable of the Good Samaritan is by the 19th-century Dutch painter, Vincent van Gogh. In his painting, van Gogh shows the Samaritan helping the victim on to his own horse before taking him to an inn. There the Samaritan paid for the victim to be taken care of.*

Parables

Jesus was once asked by a listener: 'Who is my neighbour?' Instead of answering directly, Jesus told a story about a man from Samaria, an area whose inhabitants the Jews disliked. This Samaritan helped a Jewish person who had been mugged by robbers – even though two supposedly good people had ignored the injured Jew. Jesus ended his story by asking which of the three had been 'a good neighbour' to the man who had been mugged.

Jesus told many other stories, called parables, like this one. Their point was to make his listeners think about and remember what he had taught.

In our own words

"*When I was young, I liked being told stories about Jesus. They sounded nice. Now I'm older, I read the Bible for myself and I've found that some of the things Jesus said are quite hard to do.*"

"*Jesus said we should love our enemies but when someone has said something cruel about me, I find it very hard to forgive them.*"

The teachings of the Church

In Paul's letters, written to the first Christian Churches (see page 17), Paul taught that Jesus was 'God made flesh' or 'God incarnate'. The birth of Jesus (which Christians believe is when God became a human) is called the Incarnation.

Paul also taught that the death of Jesus on the cross showed how great God's love was for all people. Not only that, Paul said, but by suffering and dying on the cross, Jesus took the consequences for the wrongdoings of all those who believe in him, and enabled them to be with God when they died. By rising from the dead and being taken back into heaven, Jesus had proved that he was indeed the Son of God and that there was a new life after death.

In one letter, Paul says that the three most important things for Christians are to have faith (or belief in God), to hope and to love generously without hoping for any reward. He goes on to say that the greatest of these three is 'love'.

The Trinity

In later years, the Church taught that God has shown himself in three ways to humankind. He has shown that he is God the loving Father and Creator; that he lived on

◀ *Jesus' rising from the dead, known as his Resurrection, is pictured here in a 15th-century prayer book that was given to Queen Isabella of Spain. After he was crucified, the body of Jesus was wrapped in cloths and placed in a tomb. Many people believe this was a cave cut into a rock face. Three days later, according to Christian belief, Jesus rose from the dead. The Resurrection has been illustrated in many ways by different artists, Here the artist has pictured the tomb as a stone coffin. He also shows an angel bringing the news to some of Jesus' followers, and their astonishment at seeing Jesus alive again.*

earth as God's Son, Jesus; and that he continues to exist in the world as God the Holy Spirit. This idea that God exists in three ways – but is still only one Being – is called the Trinity.

As time went by, the Church tried to make sure all Christians believed the same things. So creeds (or summaries of belief) were written to be said out loud by people when they became Christians. Creeds are now repeated by Christians during church services as a way of stating publicly what they believe.

Holy writings

Besides Paul's letters (or Epistles), the New Testament also includes short Epistles said to be written by other followers of Jesus such as the apostles James, Peter and John. The sayings and teachings of many other early Christians have been written down and preserved, but they do not form part of the Bible.

The Apostles' Creed
(said by Catholics and Protestants)

'I believe in God, the Father almighty,
creator of heaven and earth.
I believe in Jesus Christ, his only Son,
our Lord
who was conceived by the Holy Spirit,
born of the Virgin Mary,
suffered under Pontius Pilate,
was crucified, died and was buried;
he descended to the dead.
On the third day he rose again,
he ascended into heaven,
he is seated at the right hand of the Father,
and he will come to judge the living and
the dead.

I believe in the Holy Spirit,
the holy catholic* Church,
the communion of saints,
the forgiveness of sins,
the resurrection of the body,
and the life everlasting. Amen.'

'catholic' here means 'universal'

➤ *Many artists have used a dove as a symbol of the Holy Spirit. This picture is taken from a 15th-century French 'Book of Hours' (a medieval service book).*

3 Private and public worship

As Christians believe God is with them at all times, they do not have to go to church to pray. However, since the earliest days of the Church, they have met together (often in special buildings) to worship God and to learn more about their faith.

Private prayer

For Christians, prayer means listening and talking to God. Many Christians also believe that God 'talks' to them, not in a voice out loud that they can actually hear, but by giving them a strong feeling that they should do something in particular.

Many Christians try to remember to say prayers each morning or evening, either in their bedroom or wherever is convenient. Some families pray together before a meal. For the Christian, prayer is not just a matter of asking for things. Prayer means:

• Praising God for his greatness (Praise)

• Thanking him for his gifts such as food and health (Thanksgiving)

• Saying sorry for having done wrong things (Confession)

• Asking for his help for other people, especially loved ones and the sick (Intercession)

• Asking for help for oneself (Petition)

For their private prayers, some Christians use books of printed prayers. Many simply talk to God in their own words, as they would to a friend.

▼ An American Christian family say 'thank you' to God for food before starting a Thanksgiving dinner at their home in Austin, Texas.

The Lord's Prayer

During the Sermon on the Mount, Jesus was asked how people should pray. He taught a prayer that all Christians should say regularly to God the Father. It is known as the Lord's Prayer or the 'Our Father' (from its first two words):

'Our Father in heaven, hallowed be your name, your kingdom come, your will be done, on earth as it is in heaven.
Give us today our daily bread.
Forgive us our sins as we forgive those who sin against us.
Lead us not into temptation, but deliver us from evil.
For the kingdom, the power and the glory are yours for ever and ever. Amen.'

The exact wording of the Lord's Prayer can vary. In some versions, an old world 'trespasses' is used instead of 'sins'. The word 'Amen' is a Hebrew word meaning 'So be it' and ends most Christian prayers.

In our own words

"I try to say my prayers every evening. I like to say thank you for any good things that have happened and sorry for anything I've done wrong. I also ask God to help me. I believe he hears my prayers and answers them – but not always in the way I want. I have to trust he knows best."

▼ *Like the early Bibles, many prayer books (including this 15th-century one) were 'illuminated' with beautiful, colourful illustrations and decorative letters.*

Places of worship

Since the very early days of the Christian Church, Christians have met together to pray to and worship God. For nearly three hundred years (when it was against the law of the Roman Empire to be a Christian), they had to meet in secret. It was only after Christianity became legal that people began to build special buildings in which to meet and worship – buildings called churches.

Church buildings vary enormously. Some are very old, others modern. Some are dark and mysterious, others bright and airy. They may be beautifully decorated with stained glass windows, statues and other ornaments – or very plain and simple. They are often planned in the shape of a cross, with a tall, pointed spire or square tower at one end – pointing up to heaven. Orthodox churches are usually planned in the shape of a square cross (like a plus sign) with a dome in the centre of the roof. Older churches have bells. In the days when people had no watches, the bells told them when it was time to go to church and often rang on the hour as well. Many churches still ring hourly bells today.

Inside a church

Inside Roman Catholic and Anglican churches, the main feature is the altar or holy table, used in Holy Communion services. The altar always used to be positioned at the east end of the building, but is now sometimes in the middle. In these churches, besides seats or benches (called pews) for the people, there is usually a stand (called a lectern) from where the Bible is read aloud and a pulpit from where the priest can preach or teach the people. There may be separate pews for a

➤ *The Church of Our Lady of Health in Bangalore, India, has a tower rising high into the sky, designed to remind Christian believers of heaven.*

choir and also an organ. For Roman Catholics and Anglicans the main church of a particular region is called its cathedral. Most are very large and many are famous for the singing of their choirs.

In Orthodox churches, the altar is hidden by a screen covered with holy pictures called icons. Orthodox and Catholic churches contain many candles which are lit during services and sweet-smelling incense may be burned. The smoke from the incense is said to rise like prayers to heaven.

In Protestant churches (where preaching and Bible reading is especially important), the pulpit is often in the centre of the building. Protestants sometimes use the word chapel to describe their meeting place. A chapel can also mean a small church, or a church which is part of a school, hospital or prison.

▼ *In this Russian Orthodox Church in England, there is a screen on which there are icons (holy pictures). Through the archway in this screen can be seen the priest standing at the altar, which is mainly hidden from view.*

Church leaders

Jesus told his disciples that they were to be the servants of others; to 'minister' to their needs. These disciples became the first leaders of the Church. As the Church grew, they chose or elected other leaders. Some helpers were called deacons. The leaders of the various Churches are now known by many different titles. All those chosen to be leaders must train for several years.

Catholic, Orthodox and Anglican leaders

In the Catholic, Orthodox and Anglican churches, there are three 'orders' or ranks of leaders or clergy. The first is deacon. After one year, most deacons are made or 'ordained' priests at a service when a bishop lays hands on their heads as a sign they are being set apart for their special work. Bishops are senior priests, in charge of all the churches in one area. Each bishop has a special seat or throne in the cathedral of that area or diocese. An archbishop is even more senior, being in charge of the Church for a large part or the whole of a country.

In the Orthodox Church, senior archbishops are called patriarchs; in the Roman Catholic Church, some bishops are called cardinals. Cardinals elect the Pope, the head of the Roman Catholic Church.

In the Anglican Church, a priest who runs one (or more churches) is called a vicar or rector. A priest who works in a school, hospital, prison or the armed services is called a chaplain.

Protestant Churches

The Protestant Churches do not use the word 'priest', preferring a title such as minister or pastor. The word pastor originally meant a shepherd, someone who cares for their flock.

◄ A meeting between leaders of a small branch of the Church centred on Egypt, known as the Coptic Church. On the left is a priest, Father Boula who leads the Coptic church in Athens, Greece; on the right is the Coptic Bishop of Egypt, Bishop Gregorios. The Coptic Church was founded in Egypt by St Mark and still uses the ancient Coptic language of Egypt.

— weblinks ↖ —

For more information about the Church of England (the Anglican Church), go to www.waylinks.co.uk/series/21stcentury/Christianity

Monks and nuns

At about the time that Christianity became legal in the Roman Empire, some men and women felt it was right to live entirely for God, spending their lives in prayer, away from other people. The men became known as monks or friars; the women became known as nuns. The buildings in which monks live are known as monasteries while nuns live in convents. Originally, monks and nuns farmed their own land to provide their food and spent much time in prayer and studying the Bible, often going to seven church services every day.

Today, there are still many monks and nuns but they now often work in hospitals, schools or nursing homes. They usually make three vows or promises: to have no possessions of their own, to have no sexual relations and to be obedient to the rules of their monastery or convent.

▼ Nuns at work in St Joseph's Hospice, a home which cares for dying cancer patients in Kerala, India.

Meeting for worship

When Christians go to worship in church, they believe they are serving God. They also believe that God, through the Holy Spirit, is present in a special way during this 'service'.

There are not only different Orthodox, Roman Catholic and Protestant ways of worshipping: within each of these churches there can be many differences. What happens in an Orthodox Cathedral in Russia does not look like what happens in an English Methodist chapel or in a Baptist church in the southern states of the USA.

Christian worship usually takes place on a Sunday (the day of the Resurrection) in a church, cathedral or chapel. But it can also happen in the open air, in a football stadium, or in a simple hall. Small groups of Christians may worship in one of their own homes: what is known as a 'house church'.

Worship includes praise of God by singing holy songs known as hymns, prayer (both public and private), readings from the Bible and a sermon or talk given by the priest or minister in which he or she explains part of the Bible. In some services, sometimes called 'Services of the Word', the sermon may be quite long and the whole service will concentrate on the teachings (the 'word') of the Bible and of Jesus.

▲ *Christians in Soweto, South Africa, take part in a service of thanksgiving for blessings they have received.*

Eucharistic worship

Other services (especially in Orthodox, Roman Catholic and Anglican Churches) centre on Jesus' instruction to remember him and his Last Supper (see page 8) by sharing bread and wine. Often the bread and wine are brought by people attending the service as a thanksgiving to God. In others, small wafers are used instead of ordinary bread.

The most holy moment of the service is when the priest or minister says a prayer over the bread and wine. Some Christians believe that this is a symbol of remembrance of what happened at the Last Supper. Others, including Catholics, believe that, although the bread and wine look and taste the same, they become in some mysterious way the actual body and blood of Jesus. This service may be called the Eucharist (thanksgiving), Last Supper, Holy Communion or Mass (a title used mainly in the Roman Catholic Church).

Protestant denominations

One Protestant Church (or denomination) is the Society of Friends whose members are sometimes called Quakers. They have no priests or prayer books, and do not sing hymns. Much of their meetings for worship consists of silent prayer and meditation, broken only when one member feels he or she has something important to share.

Another Protestant denomination is the Pentecostal Church. In Pentecostal services, there is often much joyful singing, chanting and spontaneous prayer. Their worship may be led by ordinary members of the church and they believe that miracles can and do still happen. Pentecostals also believe that some of their members have the gift from God of speaking in other languages, or 'tongues', and the name Pentecostal is a reference to the Pentecost (see page 10) when it is said the disciples 'spoke in tongues'.

▼ *Worshippers gather round the altar to receive Holy Communion at a service in Tamil Nadu, in southern India.*

Christian art

The first Christians were Jews, so they followed the Jewish teaching that it was wrong to make any 'graven image', meaning that there should be no pictures or statues of holy objects or of God. Over the next few centuries, Christians began to adopt the culture of those around them and to create religious paintings, mosaics and statues. Many believed that as a church or cathedral was God's 'house on earth', it should look as splendid as possible and be the best building in the area.

Artists have painted many scenes from Bible stories – sometimes directly on to the walls and ceilings of churches, as the Italian painter Michelangelo did in the Sistine Chapel in Rome. These are called frescoes. When ordinary people were not taught to read, such pictures helped them to learn about the teachings of their religion, just as the size of large churches demonstrated the importance of God.

▲ *Part of Michelangelo's painting on the ceiling of the Sistine Chapel in Rome, Italy, a work that occupied the Italian painter from 1536 to 1541. This section shows the creation of Adam (left), the first man.*

At the time of the Reformation, many Protestant reformers felt that ornaments such as statues, stained glass windows and paintings were a distraction from the word of God. Many of these decorations were destroyed or defaced, and plainer, simpler churches and chapels were built.

Music

Music has always played an important part in Jewish worship, and the Gospels say that Jesus and his disciples sang a hymn at the Last Supper, which was part of the Jewish celebration of Pesach (Passover). Hymn-singing and the singing of the Psalms (hymns found in the Old Testament) continued to play an important part in early Christian worship, and remains an important element of most Christian services to this day.

Around the year 600CE, Pope Gregory I created the first choir school and encouraged the use of chants known as plainsong. In the 11th century, an Italian monk invented the first system for writing down musical notes.

Although Protestant reformers destroyed much of the art in their churches (see page 30), they continued to sing hymns but without instrumental accompaniments. Later,

in the 17th and 18th centuries, many new hymns were written for Christians to sing during church services, while famous composers such as J.S. Bach and W.A. Mozart wrote grand music to be sung by choirs in cathedrals and large churches.

In the last century, music became very important in Pentecostal and other Protestant churches. Many forms developed including Black Gospel music which praises God, teaches the message of the Gospel and asks for social justice.

▼ *Over the years, Christians paid for many great buildings – such as Durham Cathedral in the northeast of England. Work started in 1093CE and was completed in the remarkably short period of forty years. Because of this, the whole building is in the same style, known as Early Norman. Its impressive towers, seen here from the west, give great dignity to the cathedral.*

▲ *Roman Catholic priests lead a Christmas service in the Church of the Nativity, said to stand on the very spot where Jesus was born in Bethlehem, near Jerusalem.*

Festivals and fasts

For the first Christians, the one great festival was Sunday. Each week, it was a celebration of the Resurrection of Jesus. Soon the Church began to make a special, yearly observance of this event at Easter. Christmas and other festivals were not marked until several centuries later. Most of them celebrate events in the life of Christ and the coming of the Holy Spirit.

As Christianity spread throughout the Roman Empire, its teachers tried to persuade people to give up their old pagan celebrations. To help them do this, some Christian festivals were celebrated at the time of pagan festivals.

Christmas

Christmas is when Christians celebrate the day Jesus was born in Bethlehem. This is more than just Jesus' birthday; it is a celebration of the Incarnation, the coming of God into the world in a human body in the person of Jesus. The date of his birth is unknown, but as Jesus is sometimes called 'the light of the world' the Church decided to celebrate his birthday at the time of a pagan mid-winter festival of light (25 December). Some branches of the Orthodox Church celebrate Christmas on 6 January.

The four Sundays before Christmas are called Advent which means 'coming'. During this time, Christians prepare for the coming of Jesus at Christmas. Traditionally, it was a time of fasting or eating only a little each day. Twelve days after Christmas is the festival of Epiphany which recalls the visit of three wise men from a foreign country to the baby Jesus (sometimes mistakenly called the 'three kings').

Easter

For Christians, the most important festival is Easter. The day on which Easter Sunday falls is calculated from the lunar calendar (the cycle of the moon), and therefore changes from year to year. Before Easter is a period of forty days called Lent which, for many Christians, is a time of fasting and preparation. It begins with Ash Wednesday. On this day, some churches hold a service during which a smudge of ash is put on people's foreheads as a sign that they are sorry for the wrong things they have done.

The week immediately before Easter is called Holy Week. It begins with Palm Sunday and includes Maundy Thursday, which marks Jesus' Last Supper, and Good Friday (see pages 8-9). On Good Friday, there are special, solemn services all over the Christian world, as Christians recall the Crucifixion of Jesus.

Ascension and Pentecost

Easter is followed by forty days of rejoicing when churches are filled with flowers and, in some churches, a special Easter or 'Paschal' candle is lit. This light represents Jesus, the light of the world, and shows that Christians believe he lives, even after his Crucifixion. Then comes Ascension Day, a day which marks the last time Jesus' disciples saw him. Ten days later is Pentecost (also known as Whitsun) which marks the coming of the Holy Spirit to the faithful disciples (see page 10).

▼ *Christians carry palm branches through the streets of San Salvador in El Salvador, in memory of the entry of Jesus into Jerusalem on the very first Palm Sunday.*

Christians mark important stages of their lives with special celebrations or services. They also try to live their lives following Jesus' instruction to love other people.

Joining the Church

The Christian service of baptism is both a naming and a 'joining' ceremony. If the person being baptized (or christened) is a baby, this is the occasion when he or she is given their first or 'Christian' name. It is also the moment when the person becomes a member of the Church. Most denominations of the Church have some form of baptism. One that does not is the Society of Friends (see page 29).

The Roman Catholic, Orthodox and some Protestant Churches baptize children when they are babies. In the Russian Orthodox Church, babies are baptized when they are eight days old. In all these churches, baptism takes place at a font, often a large stone bowl. The font is usually placed near the entrance to the church building because baptism marks the entry of a person into membership of the Church. At baptism services, prayers are said and a little water is sprinkled on the person's forehead in the sign of a cross. Baptism used to be a separate, private service for the family. Now it is usually part of the main Sunday service.

▼ *A young baby is baptized in a Greek Orthodox church in the village of Tolo, near Navplion in Greece.*

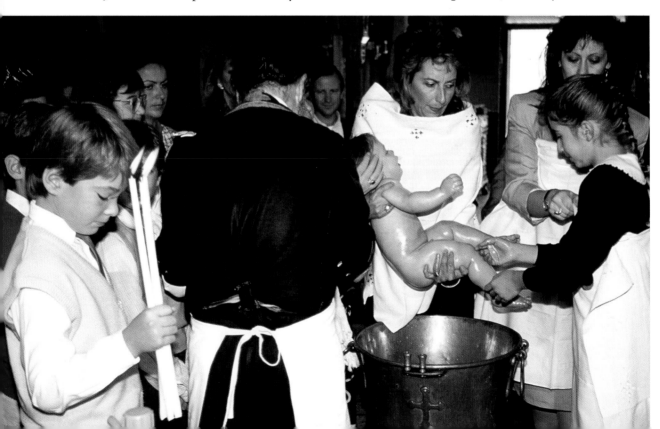

Baptism

Some Christians question whether it is right to baptize a person when they do not know what is happening to them. Jesus himself was baptized by his cousin John in the River Jordan (see box). Baptists, for example, only baptize people when they are old enough to understand what they are doing. They call this 'believers' baptism'. Instead of sprinkling a little water on their forehead, the person being baptized is immersed in a bath of water for a few seconds (just as Jesus was immersed by John). This total immersion is a sign that all past sins are being washed away.

Confirmation

In Roman Catholic and Protestant churches, there is another service called Confirmation. This is when people who were baptized as babies take upon themselves the responsibilities of being adult members of their Church. This service is led by a bishop who lays hands on the heads of those being confirmed, blessing them as full members of their Church. An adult who was not baptized as a baby may be both baptized and confirmed at about the same time.

John the Baptist

Jesus had a cousin called John who was six months older than him. When John grew up, he went to live in a desert area near the River Jordan. Many Jews came to be baptized (or 'washed of their sins') by him in that river. Before Jesus started preaching, when he was thirty, he went to be baptized by John – even though (according to Christian belief) Jesus was sinless.

➤ *Some Christians make a special journey to the River Jordan to be baptized in its waters, as Jesus was 2,000 years earlier.*

Marriage

Most Christians believe that, ideally, a man and woman should marry for life or 'till death us do part'. Only after the death of one partner is remarriage possible. This is based on Jesus' teaching that divorce (and remarriage in both partners' lifetime) is wrong: 'Whoever divorces his wife and marries another commits adultery'. Nowadays, many Christians accept divorce and remarriage because Christianity teaches that it is always possible to have a 'second chance' in life.

The marriage

Christian couples who marry want to make their promises about loving and caring for each other with God's blessing. They usually do this in a church. Their promises (called vows) to be true to each other in good and bad times ('for richer, for poorer, in sickness and in health') are nearly one thousand years old. Traditionally, the man and woman (called the groom and the bride) came to a church to make their vows – but made them to each other at the church door. They then went inside for a Holy Communion service (or Mass) and a blessing. It is only since the Reformation in the 16th century that marriages have taken place inside churches.

In the Roman Catholic and Anglican Churches the bride and groom perform the marriage ceremony: they marry one another. The priest is there only to ask (as the law requires) if there is any reason the couple should not marry each other and to declare them man and wife after they have made their vows to each other. The priest then says some prayers and blesses the marriage.

In some Orthodox churches the couple make a circular procession around the church to show that marriage has no end. They may also wear crowns to show their importance to each other.

Divorce

The Orthodox Church has allowed divorce for many centuries 'in cases of extreme distress'. The Roman Catholic Church sometimes allows marriages to be annulled (or 'made nothing') if they are proved illegal or if the couple have not had sexual relations with one another. Other Christians feel that (despite Jesus' teaching), if a marriage has failed or fallen apart in some way, it is better for the couple to divorce than to live together unhappily. They then allow the remarriage of divorced couples in church.

Celibacy

Monks and nuns never marry. This is called being celibate, which also implies absence from sexual relations. The Roman Catholic Church does not allow its priests to marry, but some feel this may change in the future.

Marriage vows

This is the marriage vow said by both the man and the woman in a modern-language Anglican marriage service:

'I, [name of man/woman] take you [name of woman/man] to be my wife/husband to have and to hold from this day forward; for better, for worse for richer, for poorer in sickness and in health, to love and to cherish, till death us do part, according to God's holy law: and this is my solemn vow.'

➤ *The groom and his bride are crowned at a Russian Orthodox marriage service in St Petersburg.*

▲ *A teenage Christian gives a present to a blind 93-year-old woman, and spends some time keeping her company.*

Christian action

In the 21st century, Christians still try to follow the 2,000-year-old teachings of Jesus to 'love your neighbour'. They also remember what he said about the hungry, the homeless and those who are ill: 'Anything you do for one of those, however humble, you do for me.' This means fighting injustice and inequality, and trying to be active in charity and good works.

Neighbourhood help

Many Christians try to help their neighbours as part of their daily lives. They may go shopping for someone who is housebound, or take someone who cannot drive to the town centre. They may garden for an old person or visit a friend or neighbour who is in hospital. Many churches organize clubs and meetings for the elderly and lonely. Some Christians do

more – by becoming prison visitors or doing voluntary work.

Giving to charity

In past times, people were expected to give one-tenth of all they earned to the Church. This was called a tithe. It sounds a lot, but in those days there was no income tax and the Church used the money to run hospitals as well as pay for church buildings and the clergy. Some Christians may still 'tithe' their income to their church, although few people now do this. However, all Christians are expected to give some money to their church and to charities.

Third World aid

Many Christian charities work with the poor and needy in their own countries. Others help those in foreign countries. Most believe this is best done not by sending clothes or tins of food abroad (although they do this at times of great disasters). Instead, many charities try to help people in developing countries to fight disease and hunger themselves. The charities do this by giving people access to tools, machinery and money, and by helping local people to acquire new skills. They also try to persuade politicians to ensure that wealth is more fairly spread between the rich and the poor countries in the world.

Revolution and war

Jesus told his followers to make peace and not to fight. Despite these words, many battles have been fought in Jesus' name over the centuries. From the 11th to the 13th centuries, Christian military expeditions, known as Crusades, were mounted to try to recapture the 'Holy Land' – the region where

Jesus lived (see page 6) – from the control of the Muslim Turks. The Crusaders came from all over western Europe, and thousands of people, Christian and Muslim, died in battles for key places such as Jerusalem.

Today, some Christians are pacifists who believe that fighting and wars are always wrong. Others believe that, occasionally, something or someone is so evil or wrong, the only way to put it right is by going to war. Often, the issues are very complicated. At the start of the 21st century, Christians were divided about whether it was right to invade Iraq to depose the Iraqi leader, Saddam Hussein. In South America, some priests have argued that revolutions are the only way to tackle the overwhelming poverty and injustice.

▼ *A charity called Christian Aid set up this scheme in Addis Ababa, Ethiopia, in 1989 to help women earn a living by processing lentils and selling them to local hotels.*

▲ *A burial at Kraal, South Africa. A part of most burial services takes place at the graveside.*

Funerals and life everlasting

Christians believe that by his Resurrection, Jesus showed that death was not an ending. They believe in a future life without end, after death. This is sometimes called 'the resurrection of the body'. Christians used to believe that the actual bodies of dead people would rise up and live again, so they were against cremation. Today, many Christians believe that what lives on is an invisible part of the human they call the soul. As a result, they do not object to cremation.

Burial

A funeral service may be very short with just a few readings and prayers. It may include hymns. Often the priest or minister will preach a sermon about the person who has died and try to comfort relatives and friends. Sometimes, the funeral may be part of a Holy Communion service. In the Roman Catholic Church, this is called a Requiem Mass.

Then comes the most solemn part of the funeral when the body is buried either in a graveyard surrounding the church, or in a cemetery. As well as speaking about death and burial, the prayers said at the graveside are also full of hope and belief in a future life.

Cremation

When a Christian is cremated, a service may be held in church before the body is taken to the crematorium, or there may be a service at the crematorium only. At the crematorium, the body is not taken out of the coffin and each coffin is burned in a special type of furnace. After an hour, the ashes are further reduced to a fine, powder-like ash and may then be buried or scattered in a place of the family's choosing.

Heaven and hell

Jesus frequently spoke about 'heaven', especially in his parables. For Christians, heaven means God's dwelling place and also of all true believers following their life on earth. Jesus also spoke of a 'Day of Judgement' when God will consider how well everyone has lived their lives. Some Christians believe this will happen for everyone when the world ends; others believe it happens for each one of us when we die.

Jesus also spoke of hell as being real and, in the past, Christian Churches have described it as a place where wicked people will suffer everlasting fires and torment. Today, many Christians place more importance on the loving and forgiving nature of God and suggest 'hell' means being separated from God – an 'absence' of God.

➤ *This is a detail from a larger painting of the Last Judgement by the 15th-century Dutch artist Rogier van der Weyden. The artist has imagined the angel Michael weighing the dead to see whether they should go up to heaven or down to hell.*

5 Christianity today

U ntil the Reformation, Christianity was largely a European religion. In more recent centuries, Christians have preached their Gospel in the Americas, Africa and Asia. The Church is now much stronger in these areas than in Europe (see page 44).

The Church around the world

From about the year 1850, Christian missionaries (the word means 'someone who is sent') began to travel in Africa, taking the teachings of Jesus to those who lived there. Other missionaries journeyed to China, India and Latin America.

In the United States, Christianity grew stronger. Thousands of pioneers who had moved west to settle went to 'camp meetings' to hear the Christian Gospel preached by a variety of Protestant denominations. In the 18th and 19th centuries, movements known as the First, Second and Third Great Awakenings led to a great strengthening in the Protestant churches. During this period, new religions (linked to Christianity) began to develop, such as the Mormon Church and the Jehovah's Witnesses. Also around this time, Americans disagreed on the question of slavery and this led to the American Civil War (1861-5). Christians were divided in the fight to end slavery, and many Christian denominations such as the Baptists, Methodists and Presbyterians were themselves split on the issue.

In 19th-century Europe, large industrial cities were growing and new Christian groups such as the Salvation Army preached the Gospel to working men and women and tried to improve their living conditions in those cities. Worldwide, by 1900, the Bible had been translated into 100 languages.

The 20th century

During the 20th century, the new Churches in Asia, Africa and Latin America grew so rapidly that there were soon far more Christians in these areas than in Europe. In Asia, countries such as South Korea and even China (where Christianity was repressed for many years) have seen a growth in the number of Christians. An Evangelical church now flourishes in Vietnam. It is in Africa, however, that most growth has been seen.

Number of Christians in Africa	
1950	25 million
1980	100 million
2000	Over 200 million

Fact box

• There are about 2,000 million Christians in the world today.

• Half of them are Roman Catholics – and half the Roman Catholics live in Central and South America.

• The Orthodox Churches have about 300 million members.

• There are more non-white Christians than white Christians.

In the United States, the Pentecostal movement began in 1906 (see page 29) Divisions began to appear at this time between Fundamentalist and Liberal Christians (see page 45). Evangelical, Fundamentalist and other Protestant Churches have become increasingly strong, encouraging lively and joyful worship. In the United States, in the year 2000, it was estimated that 44 per cent of the United States population went to church on Sundays.

Meanwhile, the number of people going to church in Europe grew smaller. By 2000, only one in ten people in Europe went to church on Sunday. Partly because of this, many Christians felt that they must try to forget past divisions and work together to spread the teachings of Jesus and to put those teachings into practice. In 1949, the World Council of Churches was formed to try to help the different Churches do this.

weblinks

For more information about the World Council of Churches, go to www.waylinks.co.uk/series/21stcentury/Christianity

➤ *Christians make their way to church for a service in Puno, Peru. The vast majority of Christians in South America are Roman Catholics.*

The Church in the 21st century

Near the end of his life on earth, Jesus told his disciples that when the Holy Spirit came to them, they would 'receive power and tell people about me everywhere'. Christians believe the Holy Spirit did come to the disciples at the first Pentecost and ever since they have believed all Christians have a duty to spread the Gospel both by what they say and what they do.

In the early years of the 21st century, Christian churches are still doing this very actively in many parts of the world. More than one-third of the world's population now describe themselves as Christian. It is the world's largest religion and still growing – not only in Latin America and Africa. Since the end of Communism in Russia, numbers have grown there too. More people are becoming Christian in China and Indonesia. In Europe, however, it is a different story. Fewer people than ever before now go to church. In Britain, the figure is 27 per cent, in France 21 per cent, and in Sweden just 4 per cent.

▼ *A woman priest leads the Easter Holy Communion service in an Episcopalian (or Anglican) church in the United States.*

When questioned, 53 per cent of Americans say that religion is very important in their lives, but only 16 per cent of Britons, 14 per cent of the French and 13 per cent of Germans answer "yes" to this question. Many more, however, say they believe in God. In recent years, Christians from Africa (especially some with Fundamentalist beliefs) have begun to travel to Europe to re-evangelize the countries that once brought them the faith.

Disagreements

Non-Christians often ask why there are so many different Churches and why Christians cannot agree among themselves. In the last fifty years, the various Churches have started to work and worship together more than they did in the past – but they still disagree about many things.

These disagreements are not just between the various Churches. People in the same Church may disagree with one another. For example, some Anglicans believe that people may remarry in church after having been divorced. Others do not. Some Roman Catholics believe that women should be allowed to

▲ *Anti-abortion and pro-choice demonstrators confront each other in front of a women's clinic in Buffalo, USA. Like many 21st-century issues, the question of abortion divides many Christians, with some strongly supporting the anti-abortion campaign, and others equally strongly believing in a woman's right to choose.*

become priests, even though their Church says they cannot.

It is now often easier to think of Christians as being divided not between Churches but between 'conservative' or 'traditional' Christians and 'liberal' Christians. Traditional Christians usually believe that what is written in the Bible is true for all time and should not be re-interpreted. If they are Roman Catholic, they accept all the teachings of their leaders, especially the Pope. Traditional Christians, especially members of some Protestant Churches, who believe in the literal truth of the Bible, are sometimes called Fundamentalists. Liberal Christians usually believe that it is right to think about what Jesus' teachings mean today, and how best to put them into practice in the modern world.

Fundamentalist Christianity has recently become a particularly powerful force in the USA. In the US presidential elections of 2004, the Christian vote helped George Bush to win a second term in office. Considerable political influence is now held by Fundamentalist Christians, and may affect crucial issues such as the right to abortion in the future.

Work outstanding

Christians have always worked to bring an end to suffering. However, most Christians are aware just how much remains to do – to bring clean water and food to all those without them, to fight disease, and to end poverty and injustice. The Christian story is far from finished.

Glossary

Advent A period of preparation that includes the four Sundays before Christmas.

apostle Describes those of Jesus' followers who first spread the teachings of Jesus.

baptism (christening) The ceremony in which a person joins the Church.

bishop The head priest of a particular area.

cathedral The main church in a particular area.

catholic Means literally 'universal' or 'worldwide'.

celibacy The state of not having sexual relations.

choir A group of singers who lead the musical part of a church or cathedral service.

Christ A title meaning 'the anointed one'.

church 1) All Christians, the whole 'family' of believers; 2) A separately organized group of Christians; 3) A building where Christians meet.

confirmation A service to renew promises made at baptism.

creed A statement or summary of beliefs.

cremation The disposal of a dead person's body by burning during a funeral service.

Crusade A medieval Christian war against Muslims.

denomination A separately organized group of Christians.

disciple A follower of Jesus.

Epistle A letter, one of several books in the New Testament.

Eucharist ('thanksgiving') Another name for Holy Communion or the Mass.

Evangelical 1) Any Christian who spreads the teaching of Jesus; 2) A Christian, usually a member of one of the Protestant Churches, who believes in the special importance of the Bible.

fast Limiting the amount of food eaten.

font A large basin used to hold holy water for baptism.

Galilee The Roman province in which Jesus grew up.

gentiles Non-Jews.

Good Friday The day three days before Easter Sunday on which Jesus was crucified.

Gospel ('good news') One of four books about Jesus in the New Testament.

Hebrew 1) A person of the Jewish race living in Biblical times; 2) The language of the Jewish people.

incarnation Being made flesh; becoming human.

lectern A desk in church from which the Bible is read.

Maundy Thursday The day before the crucifixion of Jesus on which he held his Last Supper.

Messiah A title meaning 'the chosen one' or 'the anointed one'.

miracle An event which cannot be explained by science.

missionary A person who travels, usually abroad, to teach people the faith.

New Testament The collection of Christian writings or books added to the Old Testament to form the Christian Bible.

Old Testament The Christian name for the Jewish Bible.

ordination A service at which a bishop makes a person a priest.

Orthodox ('true' or 'right') One of four east European Churches.

pagan Describes a pre-Christian religion.

Patriarch The male leader of a tribe, race or church, usually meaning one of the early Jewish leaders or the leader of an early Christian community.

parable A story with a hidden teaching or meaning.

Pope The Bishop of Rome; head or father of the Roman Catholic Church.

Protestant A member of one of the churches that separated from the Roman Catholic Church after the Reformation in the 16th century.

pulpit A stand in a church from where the sermon is given.

Reformation The 16th-century movement that led to the separation of the Protestant Churches from the Roman Church.

Resurrection Jesus' rising from the dead.

saint A person very close to God during their life.

sermon A religious talk given during a church service.

soul The inner, spirit-like part of a person said to live for ever.

spirit A being without a body.

synagogue A Jewish building for worship.

testament Means literally 'promise' or 'covenant'.

vow A promise.

Timeline

c.7-4BCE	Jesus born
CE	
c.30	Jesus crucified
46-56	Paul makes his three missionary journeys
40-100	Books of the New Testament are written
64-312	Christians persecuted by the Romans
c.100	Christianity has spread around the eastern end of the Mediterranean Sea
312	Emperor Constantine has a vision of Jesus: Christianity becomes the official religion of the Roman Empire
321	Sunday becomes a public holiday
c.400	Christianity reaches Ireland
597	Christianity brought to Canterbury in southern England
600	First choir school started; music becomes more important in Christian services
1054	Western (Catholic) and Eastern (Orthodox) Churches split
1517	Martin Luther makes public his criticisms of the Roman Catholic Church marking the start of the Reformation
1525	First Bible in the English language printed
1533	Henry VIII, King of England and Wales, breaks with the Roman Catholic Church: beginning of the Church of England, later to be part of the worldwide Anglican or Episcopalian Church
1540s	Beginnings of the Calvinist Church in Switzerland
1609	Beginning of the Baptist Church in England
1611	King James translation of the Bible printed
1639	First Baptist church in America founded at Providence on Rhode Island
1650s	Beginning of the Society of Friends (Quakers)
1682	Founding of Pennsylvania, the American state built on Quaker ideals
1784	Methodism begins as a group within the Church of England but soon becomes a separate Protestant Church
1850 onwards	Christian missionaries begin to travel widely in Africa
1865	Salvation Army founded
1900	By now the Bible has been translated into 100 languages
1906	Pentecostal Movement begins in the United States of America
1949	World Council of Churches formed to help Christian unity
2000	Celebrations held to mark 2,000 years of Christianity

Further reading

Bible Atlas by Brian Delf and Dr Stephen Motyer (Dorling Kindersley, 2001)

Great Religious Leaders: Jesus and Christianity by Alan Brown (Hodder Wayland, 2002)

The Lion Treasury of Saints by David Self (Lion Publishing, 2003)

The Roots of Christian Festivals by David Self (SPCK, 2004)

The Story of Christianity by Father Michael Collins and Matthew Price (Dorling Kindersley, 1999)

Two Thousand Years: The Christian Faith in Britain by Nicola Currie (Lion Publishing, 1999)

Index